02/09

BATS

Amy-Jane Beer

Grolier
an imprint of

www.scholastic.com/librarypublishing

Published 2008 by Grolier
An imprint of Scholastic Library Publishing
Old Sherman Turnpike, Danbury,
Connecticut 06816

For The Brown Reference Group plc
Project Editor: Jolyon Goddard
Copy-editors: Lesley Ellis, Lisa Hughes,
    Wendy Horobin
Picture Researcher: Clare Newman
Designers: Jeni Child, Lynne Ross,
    Sarah Williams
Managing Editor: Bridget Giles

Volume ISBN-13: 978-0-7172-6247-2
Volume ISBN-10: 0-7172-6247-2

Nature's children. Set 2.
    p. cm.
    Includes bibliographical references and
index.
    ISBN-13: 978-0-7172-8081-0
    ISBN-10: 0-7172-8081-0
    1. Animals--Encyclopedias, Juvenile. I.
    Grolier (Firm)
    QL49.N383 2007
    590--dc22
                        2007026928

Printed and bound in China

Contents

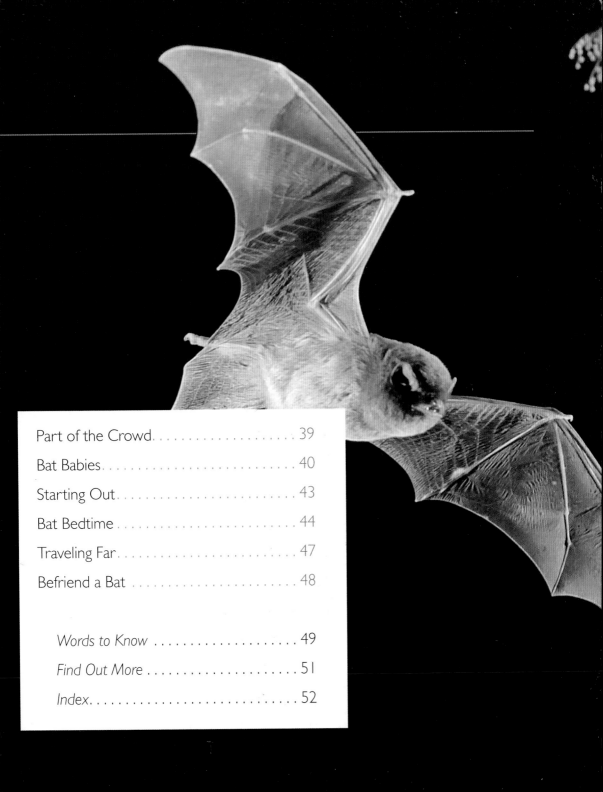

FACT FILE: Bats

Class	Mammals (Mammalia)
Order	Bats (Chiroptera)
Families	There are 18 families of bats; some with just one species, others with several hundred; the largest families are the flying foxes (184 species) and whispering bats (407 species)
Species	There are about 1,110 known species of bats
World distribution	Worldwide, except for polar regions, very remote islands, and the highest mountains
Habitat	Varies with species, from forests and rocky landscapes to farmlands and cities
Distinctive physical characteristics	Bats are the only mammals with wings that can flap; they have a furry body; most bats have big ears
Habits	Bats are nocturnal; they often roost in large colonies; some species hibernate; most of the smaller species use echolocation
Diet	Most hunt insects, others eat fruit or nectar, and a few feed on blood

Introduction

The hour after the Sun goes down is rush hour for bats. As the Sun goes down swarms of bats fill the evening sky. Bats are so quick they seem to appear from nowhere, often disappearing again just as fast. If you're lucky, you might hear them squeaking as they go by. Most adults cannot hear bats. But children have much sharper ears. If you see a bat you should not be afraid—bats will never hurt you. Bats truly are among the world's most amazing animals.

A bat flaps its wings to fly.

A flying fox
wraps itself
up in its wings
when it sleeps.

6

First Impressions

Bats have a bit of an image problem. When you mention bats, the first thing most people think of is vampires. There are bats that do feed on blood and might sometimes bite humans. They are called vampire bats but they are nothing like the monsters from horror films. Most bats are harmless though people still get scared of them. One common fear people have is that a bat might get tangled in their hair. However, bats are really good at finding their way in the dark. They are also very good at flying—a bat can change direction and dodge around obstacles at a moment's notice. So it is very unlikely that a bat will get caught in your hair!

What Is a Bat?

Bats are **mammals**. Mammals are warm-blooded, furry, or hairy, animals. Female mammals feed their babies on milk. Humans are mammals, too. We actually have more in common with bats than you might think. Both bats and humans need plenty of food to keep their body warm and active. We both need somewhere sheltered to rest and sleep. When we are young we need looking after by our parents.

Unlike humans, bats are **nocturnal**. That means they sleep during the day and come out at night. Bats are especially busy in the twilight hours, when there are many insects to eat and before the night air has become too cool.

An eastern pipistrelle
bat folds away its wings
when it rests.

This is not a bat—it's a flying squirrel. Bats flap their wings to fly. Flying squirrels use flaps of skin to glide.

Bats of Long Ago

Millions of years ago, the **ancestors** of the bats we see today were small mammals that lived in trees. These mammals ran and jumped from tree to tree with great skill. Some of them had big webbed front feet or flaps of skin down each side of the body. Those features helped the mammals glide a bit like paper airplanes— just as flying squirrels still do today. Gliding was a great way of getting around. Bats got better and better at gliding until it became flying. Today, bats are just as skillful in the air as birds and insects.

Winged Wonders

Bats look very different from other mammals because they have huge wings. But under the skin, the differences are not so great. If you look closely at a picture of a bat's wing, you can see that the wing has similar bones to those in your hand. Bats' wings are actually huge hands with webbed fingers.

The web of skin between the fingers also connects to the sides of the body. In some bats, the web connects to the back legs and tail, too, making an even bigger wing. The skin of the wing is called the **patagium** (PUH-TA-GEE-UM), or wing membrane. It is very thin and light—like the material of a parachute or a kite. The rest of the bat's body is also very light. Being light makes flight easier.

A lesser horseshoe bat spreads its wings in an attic.

13

A flying fox is active during daytime.

Great and Small

Most bats are small enough to sit in the palm of your hand. Some are really tiny. The world's smallest mammal is a bat called the bumblebee bat. Its body is about the same size as a bumblebee, although its wings are longer. This bat weighs less than a dime. Other bats are not so tiny. Most have a small, lightweight body and big wings.

There is one group of bats that grow much bigger. They are called flying foxes because they are almost the size of a fox. Most of them have a long foxlike face and red fur. But unlike real foxes, flying foxes do not eat meat. Their favorite food is sweet ripe fruit. The largest flying foxes weigh up to 3 pounds (1.3 kg) and have a wingspan of more than 5 feet (1.5 m).

Bats Everywhere

Bats live almost everywhere. There are bats on every continent, except Antarctica. There are no trees or insects in Antarctica. So there is nothing for bats to eat! On many islands, bats are the only mammals that got there without help from humans. Bats could fly to islands long before humans had invented boats or planes. Even the islands of Hawaii—thousands of miles from any other land—have bats.

Bats live in all sorts of places, or **habitats**. Some types of bats hide away in holes or tiny cracks in trees. Others, such as flying foxes, hang out in plain view. Bats often use caves because they are sheltered from the weather. Bats don't mind the dark at all. To a bat, a building is much like a cave—sometimes with the advantage of being nice and warm, too!

This cave on the island
of Bali is home to
Geoffroy's rousette bats.

A common vampire bat has small eyes.

18

Blind as a Bat?

You've probably heard the saying, "as blind as a bat." It's true that bats can't see as well as most humans. They are certainly not blind, however. Their small eyes work just fine. So why do people assume bats can't see? Maybe it's because bats live in the dark or perhaps because of the way they flit about, changing direction all the time. It can look as though a bat is lost or confused. Don't be fooled—that zigzagging bat knows exactly where it is going!

It would make much more sense to say, "as colorblind as a bat." Bats cannot see colors. Their world is all in shades of gray. That is why plants that use bats to transport their **pollen** have big white flowers. They are easier for bats to see than colored blooms.

Hear, Hear!

The ears of some bats are huge. Having big ears helps collect sound. That is why people put their hand to their ear when they are trying to hear something quiet or a long way off—the hand directs the sound into the ear.

Bats understand sound waves much better than humans. They use their hearing to build a "sound picture" of the world around them. If you shout into an empty room or a tunnel, you hear your voice echo back. Bats do the same thing, only much better. Their "shouts" are very high-pitched calls. Both the calls and the echoes are almost impossible for humans to hear, but bats pick them up loud and clear. Bats can hear the tiny echoes from objects as small as leaves and insects. From the echo bats can tell exactly where the object is. This amazing skill is called **echolocation** (EH-KOH-LOH-KAY-SHUN).

A bat's huge ears
collect sounds.

A short-tailed
noseleaf bat
hunts for prey.

Funny Face

Bats that use echolocation often have very big ears. Sometimes the ears are bigger than the rest of the head. That tells you something about how important good hearing is for a bat.

In addition to very large ears, some bats have another strange feature on the face that helps make echolocation more effective. The leaf-nosed bats have a fleshy, round or leaf-shaped structure around their nose. This structure is called the **noseleaf**. It usually has no fur, just bare skin. The noseleaf helps direct the sounds a bat makes for echolocation. The noseleaf acts a bit like the wide end of a trumpet or other brass musical instrument. This shape allows the bat to blast out calls that travel a long way.

Bat Detective

Bats are difficult animals to observe because most come out at night, spend the day hidden away, and fly very fast. People wishing to study bats often enlist the help of a little black box of electronics called a bat detector. These handy gadgets have a microphone that picks up bat calls. The bat detector then slows down the calls so that the high-pitched squeaks sound like low-pitched clicks. That allows a person investigating bats—a bat detective—to hear their noises much more easily. Different types of bats make different sorts of clicks. With a bit of practice, a bat detective can tell which kind of bat flew over her or his head just by listening!

Midair Refueling

Flying uses a lot of energy. So bats have to eat often. A bat that eats insects might have to catch thousands each night to fuel itself. On average, a bat eats about one-third of its body weight every day. If humans had to eat the same amount, we'd hardly have time to do anything else!

Most bats find their food while they are flying. Flying is a very quick way of getting around. Bats often sleep in one place, but travel each night to feed in another location several miles away. It's worth traveling to find a really good feeding spot. There, the bat can spend hours vacuuming up gnats or mosquitoes at a rate of 800 or more an hour!

A greater horseshoe bat
swoops in on a moth.

Hawker or Gleaner?

Insect-eating bats have two styles of hunting. Some snatch insects that are flying in the air. This hunting style is called **hawking**. It is similar to how some birds of prey, such as hawks and eagles, catch **prey**. Hawking requires skill and some fancy flying. The bat might grab the insect with its mouth or feet. Some bats even use their tail to scoop the insect from the air.

The other hunting style is called **gleaning**. When a bat senses its prey resting on a leaf or perhaps on the trunk of a tree, it uses a combination of swooping and hovering to bring itself within striking distance. Then the bat grabs the insect with its feet or mouth.

Both hawkers and gleaners often take their prey to a favorite perch to eat. The ground under a bat's feeding perch is often covered with the torn off wing cases of beetles and crumbly bat droppings, or **guano**.

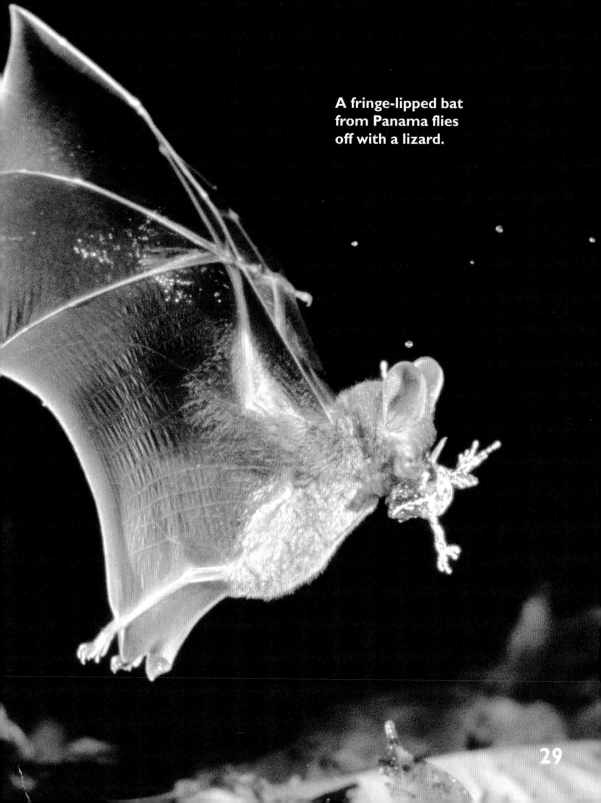

A fringe-lipped bat
from Panama flies
off with a lizard.

A vampire bat hangs from the wall of a cave in South America.

Bloodthirsty Bats

Vampire bats live in South America. These real-life vampires sneak up on large animals such as horses and goats while they are asleep. The bats crawl on all fours over the animal until they find a patch of bare skin, such as an ear. Then the bats use their razor-sharp teeth to make a small cut. Vampire bats are so careful that the sleeping animal usually does not even stir.

The small cut would normally start to heal immediately. But a vampire bat's saliva contains a chemical that stops the blood from clotting. The bat then laps up the blood that leaks out of the wound. The loss of blood is not usually enough to do the victim any lasting harm. The only real danger is if the wound becomes infected with a disease such as rabies. Rabies is a deadly disease that can be spread by bats. It is passed on when an infected bat bites another animal.

Flower Power

Many bats are vegetarians and do not eat insects or other animals. Vegetarian bats eat only items produced by plants. Flying foxes are sometimes called fruit bats because they love fruit, especially really soft ripe fruit that contains a lot of sugar.

Many smaller bats eat pollen and **nectar** from flowers. The bats do these plants a favor by carrying pollen from flower to flower just like bees and butterflies. Many types of plants depend completely on bats to do this important job for them. These plants have flowers that open at night instead of during the day. The flowers are usually white and have a strong smell. The bright white color and strong odor make it easy for bats to find the flowers.

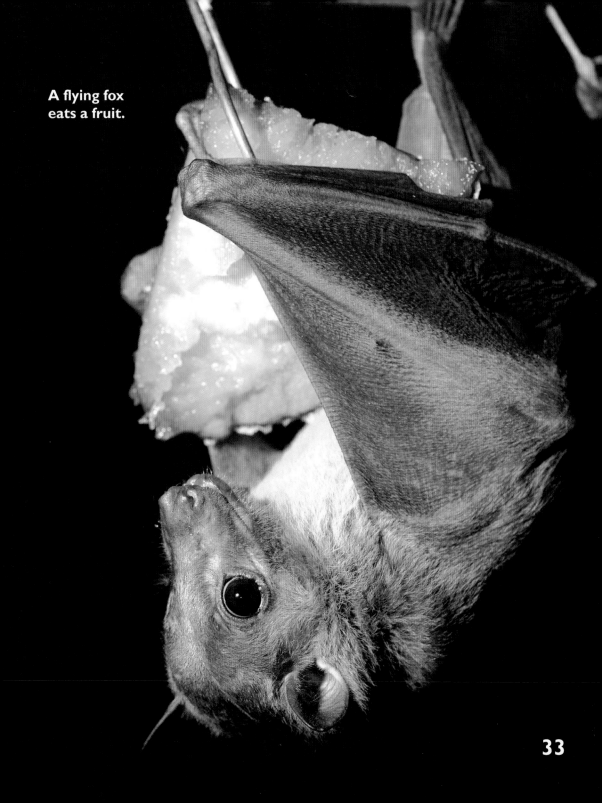

A flying fox
eats a fruit.

A bat's hooklike toes grip tightly when it hangs upside down.

Hanging Out

Bats have very small back legs. They lack the big muscles you see in the legs of land animals. If they land on the ground, bats crawl around on their hind legs and front wings almost helplessly. Worse still, bats cannot usually take off from the ground. They need to launch from a high perch. So when a bat needs to rest, it finds a sheltered spot called a **roost**. There, the bat hangs upside down by its back feet. It can relax in this upside-down position as long as it likes. A bat's ten toes form natural hooks, so the bat doesn't have to use any energy to hold on. Some bats have suckers on the soles of their feet. These suckers also help the bat to hold onto a roost.

Home to Roost

Different bats choose different kinds of places to roost. Caves and tree holes are popular because they are sheltered from wind and rain and from the eyes of **predators**. These places also have rough surfaces that the bats can cling to. Flying foxes are big enough to have few enemies. They roost in noisy gangs, or groups, in the branches of trees, often in plain view.

Some bats roost alone. But most bats roost in groups. Sometimes, these groups are enormous. The roosts are like vast bat cities with thousands, even millions, of bats living together. In the world's largest roosts, there can be up to 20 million bats sharing huge caves! The floors of these caves are covered in several feet of guano.

Flying foxes
roost in a tree
in Australia.

Observers watch as bats swarm in Austin, Texas.

Part of the Crowd

At certain times of the year, some bats of the same kind come together to form huge midair crowds called swarms. That is when the bats really show off their flying skills. There can be thousands, even millions of bats, in a swarm. But the bats never seem to collide.

There are many reasons for swarming. Young bats probably do it to help them get a feel for the local area before they venture out alone. Adult bats sometimes swarm in spring after they come out of **hibernation**. That probably helps them get their bearings again. Bats also swarm in fall, when they are ready to **mate**. Swarming gives males and females a chance to check one another out, before mating.

Bat Babies

Bats mate in fall. The females are pregnant through winter, and the babies are born in spring. When the time comes for the young to arrive, the mothers gather in female-only roosts.

Each bat mother usually produces just one large baby. A newborn bat can weigh up to a quarter of its mother's weight. Some bats give birth while hanging upside down. Others turn the right way up and hang from their thumbs to give birth. Those bats use their webbed tail to catch the baby as it is born. The baby knows how to cling on. It immediately crawls to a safe position on the mother's front. From there, the baby can reach the nipple near her armpit to feed on milk. The mother wraps her wings around the baby to keep it safe and warm.

A flying fox mother cuddles her baby.

A common long-eared bat carries its young in flight.

Starting Out

Mother bats need to keep their strength up if they are to produce milk for their young. To do that, they must still go out to find food for themselves. To begin with, the baby travels with its mother. The baby clings tightly to its mother's fur as she flies. But after just a few weeks, the baby is so heavy its mother can no longer carry her offspring. She leaves the baby hanging in the roost while she goes out. Other mothers in the roost hang their babies in the same place. The young cluster for warmth and comfort.

After as little as five or six weeks, the young bats are ready to try flying. They start by exercising their wings, flapping while upside down on the perch. The young bats are nervous at first. But once the youngsters get up the courage to let go, they find flying comes naturally. They start with short flights. Gradually the flights get longer as their strength increases.

Bat Bedtime

Bats that live in tropical parts of the world can usually find plenty to eat throughout the year. The tropics are hot and sunny all year round. Life is more difficult for bats that live in cooler regions. If a bat cannot find enough food every day, it begins to starve. Away from the tropics, there are few insects or flowers in winter. It can be almost impossible for bats to find enough to eat.

To avoid starving, many bats in cooler regions hibernate in winter. Hibernation is like a very long, deep sleep that lasts several months. The bat lets its body become cold, and its heart rate slows to just one or two beats a minute. In this state, the bat uses hardly any energy. This way, the bat can survive without food until spring.

A whiskered bat
hibernates in a
cave in Europe.

45

In winter this female Schreiber's long-fingered bat migrates to caves where she gives birth and raises her young.

Traveling Far

You've probably heard about birds, such as swallows and geese, that fly south for winter. Or perhaps you've heard about the great journeys made by some other animals such as bison or wildebeest. These amazing round trips are called **migrations**. They usually happen at the same time each year. Some bats migrate, too. They often do it for the same reason that other bats hibernate in winter—to avoid the long cold season when food is scarce. Some female bats also migrate to find somewhere to give birth and raise their young.

Migrating bats usually fly at night, but they use the same routes as birds. They have a built-in compass that tells them the right way to go—even if the bats have never made the trip before. Migrating bats also use landmarks such as rivers and mountains to find their way. Amazingly, many roost in the same cave or tree each year.

Befriend a Bat

It's a shame that so many people are afraid of bats, because these wonderful animals really need friends. Many types of bats are rare, and without help and protection they will die out.

What will you think the next time you see a bat? Will you run around in a panic or shriek in fright for no good reason? Or will you feel a thrill at seeing such an amazing animal? If your ears are still young, you might even have the great privilege of hearing those tiny squeaks as the bat flies by.

If you become a friend to bats, you will find there are many more people like you. Look at the web sites listed at the end of this book to find out more about bats that live near you and how you can get to know and help them.

Words to Know

Ancestors   Early types of existing species.

Echolocation   The way most bats sense the world around them and find food.

Gleaning   A way of hunting in which prey are picked off leaves or other surfaces.

Guano   Bat, or seabird, droppings.

Habitats   Types of places that plants or animals live.

Hawking   Hunting by grabbing other animals in flight.

Hibernation   A deep sleeplike state some bats enter for winter to survive the cold and hardships.

Mammals   Animals with fur or hair that feed their young on milk.

Mate	To come together to produce young.
Migrations	Long journeys, usually made at the same time each year.
Nectar	A sugary liquid produced by flowers.
Nocturnal	Active at night.
Noseleaf	The fleshy structure on the face of some bats used to direct sound.
Patagium	The thin skin of a bat's wing.
Predators	Animals that hunt other animals for food.
Prey	An animal hunted by other animals.
Pollen	A substance produced by flowers to produce seeds.
Roost	A place where bats rest or raise young.

Find Out More

Books

Graham, G. L. *Bats of the World*. Golden Guides. New York, New York: St. Martin's Press, 2001.

Kalman, B. and K. Lundblad. *Endangered Bats*. Ontario, Canada: Crabtree Publishing, 2006.

Web sites

All About Bats
www.enchantedlearning.com/subjects/mammals/bat
Fun facts about bats.

Bat Conservation International
www.batcon.org
A great introduction to the amazing world of bats.

Organization for Bat Conservation
www.batconservation.org
Information about bats and how to protect them.

Index